Indian and Mediterranean Fish Recipes

Gain creativity, tastefulness and a perfect weight balance, with these delicious, quick and easy recipes for beginners. Expand your knowledge to the worldwide and heal your body and mind. Learn how to do step by step and keep a great quality, maintaining a low budget

Ernest Pescara

Table of Contents

Welcome, dear!

This is my offer to your cooking style.

This cookbook is the realization of my research on how to eat tasty and healthy food at the meantime.
My purpose is to increase your energies and to let you live a lighter life, without the junk of the globalised kitchen.

In here, you'll find my knowledge on how to create delicious dishes with Indian and Mediterranean fishes.

Jump into a worldwide discovery of good food and natural-feed animals, with many recipes for a varied diet.

Nevertheless, you'll learn new techniques, discover tastes of all around the world and improve your skills.
Let yourself be inspired by the worldwide traditions, twisted by a proper chef.

Each of these dishes is thought to:

1 – Let you understand how to work with Indian and Mediterranean fish

This majestic animal is presented in various dishes of different cultures, to show you how the same ingredient can change from dish to dish.

2 – Balance your weight with different cooking methods

As soon as you learn different ways to cook your fish, you'll discover an entire world of new ideas.
Indian and Mediterranean fish will never bore you again!

3 – Amaze your friends starting from the smell

Once your friends will come to dinner, they will be in love with your food even before to see your creation.

Indian Fish Recipes

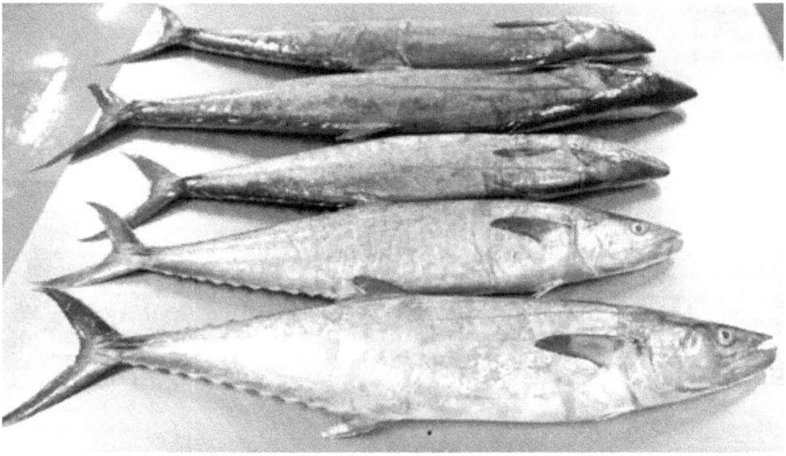

Garlic Lime Sea Bass

Serves 4 pax

Ingredients

- 1 large onion, chopped
- 2 to 3 tablespoons lime juice
- 1 tablespoon spicy brown mustard
- 1/4 teaspoon salt
- 1/4 teaspoon pepper
- 1 whole garlic bulb
- 1 teaspoon olive oil
- 1/4 cup butter, cubed
- 4 sea bass or grouper fillets (8 ounces each)

Procedure

1. From garlic, remove papery outer skin; don't separate or peel cloves. Cut off top of bulb; brush oil. Use heavy-duty foil to wrap; bake till soft for 30-35 minutes at 425°. Cool for 10-15 minutes.
2. Lower heat to 350°. Melt butter in a small saucepan. Into pan, squeeze softened garlic; mix in pepper, salt, mustard, lime juice and onion. Mix and cook till onion is tender on medium heat.
3. Put fillets into 11 x 7-in. ungreased baking dish; put onion mixture over.
4. Bake till fish easily flakes with a fork for 30-35 minutes, uncovered.

Sea Tikka Kebabs

Serves 5 pax

Ingredients

- 2 fresh green chile peppers, such as serrano, stemmed, seeded, and thinly chopped
- 1 cup Tikka Marinade of your choice
- 10 metal or bamboo skewers, soaked in water at least 30 minutes
- Salad greens, lime or lemon, and tomato wedges, scallion whites, thinly chopped
- 1 tablespoon melted butter
- 2 pounds firm white fish fillets, such as sea bass, halibut, or orange roughy, approximately 1 inch thick, cut into 1 inch pieces

Procedure

1. Ready the marinade. Next, place the fish pieces in a big non-reactive container, put in the marinade (saving approximately 1/4 cup to use for basting as you grill), and mix thoroughly, ensuring all the pieces are coated thoroughly. Cover and marinate in the refrigerator, approximately two hours.
2. Thread fish pieces on skewers (four to five pieces per skewer) and discard the used marinade.
3. Preheat a grill using moderate to high heat to 375°F to 400°F and grill, turning and rotating the skewers, until mildly charred and tender, approximately ten minutes. Moisten once in a while with the reserved marinade. During the last minute of the cook, baste with the melted butter.
4. Move to a platter lined with salad greens. Garnish with fresh lime or lemon and tomato wedges, scallion whites, and green chile peppers.
5. Serve.

Sesame Tikka Marinade

Serves 5 pax

Ingredients

- 1/2 teaspoon Asian sesame oil
- 1/2 teaspoon cayenne pepper, or to taste
- 1 teaspoon Chaat Masala
- 1/4 cup non-fat plain yogurt, whisked until the desired smoothness is achieved
- 1/4 teaspoon ground asafoetida
- 2 tablespoons Tamarind Paste
- 2 teaspoons garam masala
- 1 teaspoon salt, or to taste
- 1 teaspoon sesame seeds, dry-roasted
- 2 tablespoons Basic Ginger-Garlic Paste

Procedure

1. Ready the chaat masala, sesame seeds, ginger-garlic paste, and the tamarind paste.
2. In a large non-reactive container, combine all the ingredients, except the chaat masala and sesame seeds.
3. Sprinkle the chaat masala and sesame seeds as a decoration, just before you serve.

Fish Kebabs

Serves 5 pax

Ingredients

- 1/2 cup cornmeal
- 1/2 cup rice flour
- 1/2 teaspoon ground fenugreek seeds
- 1/8 teaspoon ground asafoetida
- 1/4 teaspoon ground turmeric
- 2 pounds any firm white fish fillets, such as sea bass or cod, approximately 1-inch thick, cut into 3-inch pieces
- 2 cups peanut oil for deep-frying
- 2 teaspoons hot red pepper flakes, or to taste
- 5 Lemon wedges
- 1/3 cup water
- 1 tablespoon fresh lemon juice
- 1 teaspoon ground cumin seeds
- 1 teaspoon salt, or to taste
- 2 tablespoons finely chopped fresh cilantro, including soft stems

Procedure

1. Put the fish pieces in a big non-reactive container, put in the salt and turmeric, and mix thoroughly. Cover and marinate in the fridge one to two hours.
2. In a moderate-sized container, combine the rice flour, red pepper flakes, cumin, fenugreek, asafoetida, and just sufficient water to form a thick paste.
3. Heat the oil in a wok or large skillet using high heat until it registers 350°F to 375°F on a frying thermometer or until a small piece of fish dropped into the hot oil bubbles and instantly rises to the top.
4. Smear each piece of fish with the rice flour paste, dredge it in the corn meal and cautiously add to the hot oil, adding as many pieces as the wok can hold simultaneously.
5. Fry, turning as required, until they are golden and crisp, approximately two to three minutes. Move to paper towels to drain.
6. Move to a serving dish, garnish with lemon wedges and cilantro before you serve.

Fried Fish

Serves 5 pax

Ingredients

- 1 tablespoon Basic Ginger-Garlic Paste
- 1 tablespoon mustard oil
- 1/8 teaspoon ground asafoetida
- 1/4 cup chickpea flour
- 2 tablespoons fresh lime juice
- 2 tablespoons peanut oil
- 6 scallions, cut into 1-inch diagonal pieces
- 5 Lemon wedges
- 3/4 teaspoon ajwain seeds
- 1 teaspoon Chaat Masala
- 1 teaspoon ground paprika
- 1 teaspoon salt, or to taste
- 2 pounds any firm white fish fillets, such as sea bass, halibut, cod, or swordfish, approximately 1 inch thick, cut into 3-inch pieces

Procedure

1. Put the fish in a big non-reactive container, put in the salt and lime juice, and toss softly to mix. Cover and marinate in the fridge 30 to 60 minutes. Drain thoroughly.
2. To the fish, put in the chickpea flour, ginger-garlic paste, ajwain seeds, paprika, and asafoetida, and mix, ensuring all the pieces are coated thoroughly with the marinade. Cover and marinate at least 2 and maximum four hours in a fridge.
3. Heat both the oils in a big non-stick skillet using moderate to high heat and put in the fish pieces very cautiously (the oil may splatter).
4. Cook, turning once, until both sides are golden and the fish is just flaky and opaque inside, approximately four minutes per side.
5. Move to a platter, sprinkle the scallions and chaat masala on top, garnish with the lemon wedges before you serve.

South Style Fried Fish

Serves 5 pax

Ingredients

- 1/3 cup rice flour
- 1 cup coconut oil or peanut oil for deep-frying
- 1 tablespoon fresh lemon juice
- 1/8 teaspoon ground asafoetida
- 2 teaspoons cayenne pepper, or to taste
- 4 to 6 lemon wedges
- 1/8 teaspoon ground turmeric
- 1 teaspoon salt, or to taste
- 2 pounds any small firm fish, such as trout, cut on both sides of the center bone, bone discarded, and cut into 3-inch pieces

Procedure

1. Put the fish pieces on a large platter, skin side down. Sprinkle with the salt and marinate for approximately half an hour in a fridge.
2. In a flat dish, combine the rice flour, cayenne pepper, turmeric, and asafoetida. Using a paper towel, dry each piece of fish, then dredge it in the rice flour mixture.
3. Heat the oil in a big non-stick skillet using moderate to high heat until it achieves 325°F to 350°F on a frying thermometer or until a small piece of fish dropped into the hot oil takes about fifteen to twenty seconds before it rises to the top.
4. Standing far from the wok, put in the fish, one piece at a time, adding as many as the wok will hold simultaneously without crowding, and fry, flipping the pieces around with a slotted spatula, three to five minutes per batch.
5. Move to a tray coated using paper towels to drain, then move to a serving platter.
6. Sprinkle the lemon juice on top, garnish with lemon wedges before you serve.

Broiled Swordfish

Serves 5 pax

Ingredients

- 1 tablespoon black mustard seeds, crudely ground
- 1 tablespoon fresh lime or lemon juice
- 1 teaspoon ground turmeric
- 1 large clove fresh garlic, peeled
- 1/2 teaspoon ground ajwain seeds
- 1/2 teaspoon salt, or to taste
- 1 fresh green chile pepper, such as serrano, stemmed
- 4 quarter-size slices peeled fresh ginger
- 6 (1-inch-thick) swordfish steaks or fillets (6 to 8 ounces each)
- 2 tablespoons finely chopped fresh cilantro
- 2 tablespoons heavy cream
- 2 tablespoons mustard oil or peanut oil

Procedure

1. Put the fish in a big non-reactive container, put in the turmeric and salt, and mix thoroughly. Cover using plastic wrap and marinate at least 1 and maximum one day in a fridge.
2. In a small food processor or a blender, combine and pulse the ginger, garlic, and green chile pepper until minced.
3. Put in the oil, cream, lemon juice, mustard seeds, and ajwain seeds and process once more until a smooth paste is achieved. Combine with the fish, ensuring all steaks are coated thoroughly with the mixture. Cover and refrigerate one hour.
4. Preheat the broiler. Put the fish in a lightly oiled broiler-safe baking dish and broil four to five inches from the heating element until the top is lightly browned, approximately five minutes.
5. Turn the pieces over and broil until the other side is lightly browned, approximately four to five minutes, or until the thickest part of the fish is opaque when checked with a knife. Move to plates, sprinkle the cilantro on top before you serve.

Masala Fish

Serves 5 pax

Ingredients

- 1/2 teaspoon ground ajwain seeds
- 1/2 teaspoon salt, or to taste
- 1 tablespoon Basic Garlic Paste
- 1/4 teaspoon cayenne pepper, or to taste
- 1/4 teaspoon freshly ground black pepper
- 1/2 teaspoon garam masala
- 1 tablespoon ground paprika
- 3 tablespoons fresh lemon or lime juice
- 2 tablespoons mustard oil or peanut oil
- 1 tablespoon Tamarind Paste
- 2 pounds firm white fish fillets, such as halibut, cod, or catfish, approximately
- 1/2 inch thick, cut into 3-inch pieces

Procedure

1. Ready the garlic and tamarind pastes. Put the fish in a large, flat dish. combine the garlic paste, all the spices and salt, and rub well over the fillets, ensuring each one is coated thoroughly.
2. Cover and marinate in the fridge for minimum 1 and maximum four hours.
3. Heat 2 tablespoons oil in a big non-stick skillet using high heat until smoking, approximately two minutes.
4. Cautiously place the fillets in the pan in a single layer and cook until turn blacked on the bottom, approximately five minutes.
5. Drizzle the rest of the oil on top of the fish fillets and turn them over. Cook, pressing the top turn blacked side softly with the back of a spatula to flatten, and cook until the other side is thoroughly browned and the inside just flaky and opaque, approximately four minutes.
6. Move to a serving dish, drizzle the lemon juice on top before you serve hot.

Grilled Sea Bass

Serves 5 pax

Ingredients

- 1 teaspoon ground paprika
- 1 teaspoon salt, or to taste
- 2 tablespoons Basic Ginger-Garlic Paste
- 1 tablespoon melted butter of vegetable oil
- 1 teaspoon crudely crushed ajwain seeds
- 1 teaspoon Chaat Masala
- 3 teaspoons ground cumin
- 2 tablespoons fresh lime or lemon juice
- 2 cups mixed baby greens
- 5 pounds Chilean or Pacific sea bass fillets, approximately 1 inch thick, cut into 2 inches pieces
- 2 tablespoons Coconut Milk
- 5 Lime wedges

Procedure

1. Ready the coconut milk, ginger-garlic paste, and chaat masala.
2. Next, in a big nonreactive container, combine all the ingredients, except the fish, greens, chaat masala, and lime wedges.
3. Put in the fish and mix, ensuring all the pieces are coated thoroughly. Cover using plastic wrap and marinate in the refrigerator, at least 4 and maximum 1two hours.
4. Preheat the grill to 400°F or place a grill pan using high heat. Moisten the grill or grill pan with oil to stop the fish from sticking to the grill.
5. Next, place the marinated pieces on the grill or in the grill pan (or use a grilling basket) and cook, flipping over once or twice, until the fish pieces are opaque and just flaky inside and mildly charred on the outside, approximately five to seven minutes.
6. Line a platter with baby greens and move the fish to rest on the greens.
7. Sprinkle the chaat masala on top before you serve hot with lime wedges on the side.

Sea Bass with Yogurt and Cilantro Sauce

Serves 5 pax

Ingredients

- 1 tablespoon ground black mustard seeds
- 1 teaspoon Chaat Masala
- 1 teaspoon salt, or to taste
- 3 green chile peppers, stemmed
- 1/4 teaspoon ground turmeric
- 1/2 teaspoon ground paprika
- 1 cup non-fat plain yogurt, whisked until the desired smoothness is achieved
- 2 tablespoons vegetable oil
- 3 tablespoons fresh lemon juice
- 2 pounds sea bass, halibut, or any firm white fish fillets, approximately 3/4 inch thick, cut into 1-inch pieces
- 1 large bunches fresh cilantro (about 5 ounces each), crudely chopped
- 8 quarter-size slices peeled fresh ginger
- A few cilantro sprigs

Procedure

1. Ready the chaat masala. Put the fish pieces in a container and softly stir in the oil,
2. mustard seeds, and turmeric. Put the yogurt in a separate serving container.
3. Put the cilantro Using a food processor or a blender, put in the lemon juice, ginger, green chile peppers, paprika, and salt, and process to make a fine purée.
4. Divide the purée into 2 portions. Mix 1 portion into the fish. Cover using plastic wrap and marinate at least 2 and maximum one day in a fridge.
5. Mix the second portion into the yogurt, along with the chaat masala, to make a saucy chutney. Cover and refrigerate until needed.
6. Heat a large non-stick skillet using moderate to high heat, and cook the fish, flipping over once or twice, until just flaky and golden outside.
7. Move to a serving dish, drizzle approximately 1/2 cup yogurt sauce on the fish, garnish with the cilantro sprigs before you serve hot with the rest of the yogurt sauce on the side.

Spiced Tuna

Serves 2 pax

Ingredients

- 1 tablespoon finely chopped fresh cilantro, including soft stems
- 1 tablespoon peeled minced fresh ginger
- 1/2 teaspoon salt, or to taste
- 1 can white chunk tuna packed in water, drained
- 1 teaspoon black mustard seeds
- 1 teaspoon oil
- 7 fresh green curry leaves

Procedure

1. Heat the oil in small-sized non-stick skillet using moderate to high heat and put in the mustard seeds; they should splatter when they touch the hot oil, so cover the pan until the splattering diminishes.
2. Swiftly put in the ginger and curry leaves, cook 1 minute, then put in the tuna and salt and cook, stirring, another minute.
3. Move to a serving dish, garnish with the cilantro before you serve.

Tomatoes and Fish

Serves 5 pax

Ingredients

- 1/2 cup finely chopped fresh cilantro
- 1/2 teaspoon salt
- 1 medium whole firm fish, such as pomfret, mackerel, trout, or catfish, cleaned, with head and tail intact, washed well and patted dry
- 1/8 teaspoon ground asafoetida
- 1/4 cup vegetable oil
- 1/4 teaspoon ground turmeric
- 3 fresh green chile peppers, stemmed
- large cloves fresh garlic, peeled
- 1 piece dried kokum, crudely chopped
- 1 small onion, crudely chopped
- 1 tablespoon ground coriander
- 1 teaspoon ground cumin
- 1 teaspoon ground fenugreek seeds
- 5 small firm tomatoes, cut into 6 wedges each
- 1 quarter-size slices peeled fresh ginger

Procedure

1. Using a knife, make long and deep diagonal cuts, 2 inches apart, on both sides of the fish.
2. Using a blender or a food processor, combine and pulse the onion, garlic, ginger, green chile peppers, and kokum until the desired smoothness is achieved.
3. Put in the coriander, fenugreek, cumin, salt, turmeric, and asafoetida and process once more until a smooth paste is achieved.
4. Spread the paste liberally on the fish, ensuring to stuff some into the cuts. Save any leftover paste. Cover and marinate the fish in the refrigerator, at least 2 and maximum four hours.
5. Heat the oil in a big non-stick skillet using moderate to high heat and very cautiously (there will be some splattering, so keep the lid handy) Put in the fish.
6. Fry, turning once, until a golden color is achieved and flaky, approximately five minutes per side.

7. Move to a serving platter. Drain most of the oil, leaving approximately 1 teaspoon oil in the skillet.
8. Add the rest of the onion paste to the skillet and cook, stirring, approximately one minute.
9. Put in the tomatoes and cilantro and cook until the tomatoes are slightly soft, approximately one minute.
10. Use to garnish the fish before you serve hot.

Grilled Tikka Marinade

Serves 5 pax

Ingredients

- 1/2 teaspoon crudely ground ajwain seeds
- 1 teaspoon cayenne pepper, or to taste
- 1 teaspoon salt, or to taste
- 3 tablespoons fresh lemon juice or distilled white vinegar
- 2 tablespoons Basic Ginger-Garlic Paste
- 1/4 cup non-fat plain yogurt, whisked until the desired smoothness is achieved
- 1/4 teaspoon ground turmeric
- 3 teaspoons garam masala
- 3 teaspoons ground cumin

Procedure

1. Ready the ginger-garlic paste.
2. Mix all the ingredients well in a big non-reactive container.

Sour Fish

Serves 5 pax

Ingredients

- 1/2 teaspoon salt, or to taste
- 1 cup water
- 1 large onion, cut in half along the length and thinly chopped
- 1/4 teaspoon crudely ground ajwain seeds
- 1/2 cup fresh curry leaves, crudely crumpled
- 1/2 teaspoon garam masala
- 1 large tomato, finely chopped
- 5 tablespoons distilled white vinegar
- 3 tablespoons vegetable oil
- 3 fresh green chile peppers, minced with seeds
- 2 teaspoons ground black mustard seeds
- 2 pounds any firm white fish fillets, such as sea bass, halibut, cod, or swordfish, approximately 3/4-inch thick, cut into 2-inch pieces

Procedure

1. Heat the oil in a big non-stick wok or saucepan using moderate to high heat and put in the mustard seeds; they should sizzle when they touch the hot oil. Swiftly put in the onion and cook, stirring, two minutes.
2. Put in the tomato and the green chile peppers. In a container, toss the fish pieces with ajwain seeds and salt, then place them over the tomatoes. Cover the fish well with the curry leaves.
3. Next, put in the water and vinegar, cover the pan, and cook using moderate to high heat the first two to three minutes and then over moderate heat until the fish is flaky and opaque inside, approximately eight to ten minutes. Remove most of the curry leaves and discard.
4. Move the fish to a serving dish, sprinkle the garam masala on top before you serve.

Curried Fish

Serves 5 pax

Ingredients

- 1/4 teaspoon ground paprika
- 1/2 cup non-fat plain yogurt, whisked until the desired smoothness is achieved
- 1/4 cup finely chopped fresh cilantro
- 1/4 teaspoon cayenne pepper
- 1/4 teaspoon garam masala
- 1/2 recipe Fried Onion Paste
- 1/2 teaspoon ground turmeric
- 2 pounds any firm fish fillets, such as sea bass, halibut, cod, or swordfish, approximately 3/4 inch thick, cut into 2-inch pieces
- 5 large tomatoes, finely chopped
- 1/2 teaspoon salt, or to taste
- 1 cup water
- 1 tablespoon ground coriander
- 1 teaspoon ground cumin

Procedure

1. Ready the onion paste. Put the fish in a container and cover thoroughly with the turmeric and cayenne pepper.
2. Cover using plastic wrap and marinate at least 1 and maximum one day in a fridge.
3. Ready the fried onion paste. Put the paste in a big non-stick wok or saucepan using moderate to high heat, put in the coriander, cumin, and paprika, and stir approximately one minute.
4. Put in the yogurt, slowly and gradually, stirring constantly, to stop it from curdling, and cook until it is well completely blended with the sauce, approximately three minutes.
5. Put in the tomatoes and cook until they begin to soften, approximately two minutes. Put in the fish pieces and salt and cook, stirring, until the fish is firm, approximately five minutes.
6. Put in the water and bring to a boil using high heat.

7. Decrease the heat to moderate to low, cover the pan, and simmer until the fish pieces are just flaky and opaque inside and the sauce is thick, approximately five minutes.
8. Move to a serving dish, stir in the cilantro and garam masala before you serve.

5 Spices Fish

Serves 5 pax

Ingredients

- 1 tablespoon Bengali 5-Spices (Panch-Phoran)
- 1 teaspoon cayenne pepper, or to taste
- 1/4 cup water
- 1/2 teaspoon salt, or to taste
- 3/4 teaspoon ground turmeric
- 3 tablespoons finely chopped fresh cilantro
- 2 tablespoons mustard oil or vegetable oil
- 2 pounds any firm fish fillets, such as halibut or swordfish, approximately 3/4 inch thick, cut into 2-inches pieces
- 3 cups finely chopped tomatoes

Procedure

1. Ready the 5-spice mixture. Put the fish pieces in a big non-reactive container. Put in the 1/4 teaspoon turmeric and salt and mix thoroughly, ensuring all the pieces are coated thoroughly.
2. Cover using plastic wrap and marinate in the fridge for minimum 1 and maximum four hours.
3. Heat 1 tablespoon oil in a big non-stick skillet over moderate heat and fry the fish pieces (leave any juices in the container), in 2 or 3 batches if needed, until a golden color is achieved, approximately two minutes per side. Move to a container.
4. To the container with the fish juices, put in the rest of the 1/2 teaspoon turmeric, cayenne pepper, and water and mix thoroughly to make a paste.
5. Heat the rest of the 1 tablespoon oil in the same skillet and put in the panch-phoran;
6. they should splatter when they touch the hot oil, so cover the pan until the splattering diminishes.

7. Swiftly put in the turmeric paste, stir approximately one minute, then put in the tomatoes and cook until most of the fluids vaporize, approximately five minutes.
8. Stir in the fish, plus any juices that may have accumulated, and cook over moderate heat two to three minutes to blend the flavors.
9. Move to a serving dish, sprinkle the cilantro on top before you serve.

Goan Fish

Serves 5 pax

Ingredients

- 1 cup Coconut Milk
- 1 cup water
- 1 large onion, finely chopped
- 1/4 cup finely chopped fresh cilantro
- 1/4 teaspoon ground turmeric
- 1 teaspoon coriander seeds
- 1 teaspoon cumin seeds
- 3 tablespoons Tamarind Paste
- 3 dried red chile peppers, broken into pieces
- 2 large cloves fresh garlic, minced
- 1 teaspoon salt, or to taste
- 2 pounds any firm fish fillets, such as catfish, salmon, or swordfish, approximately 1 inch thick, cut into 2-inch pieces
- 3 tablespoons vegetable oil

Procedure

1. Ready the coconut milk and tamarind paste. Heat the oil in a big non-stick wok or saucepan using moderate to high heat and cook the onion, stirring, until a golden color is achieved, approximately five minutes. Put in the garlic and stir 1 minute.
2. In a small spice grinder or coffee grinder, mix together and grind the red chile peppers, coriander, and cumin. Stir in the turmeric, then put in the spice mixture to the onions and cook, stirring, approximately two minutes.
3. Put in the water and coconut milk and bring to a quick boil, stirring, using high heat. Decrease the heat to medium and simmer approximately five minutes. Put in the tamarind paste and salt and simmer another minute.
4. Put in the fish pieces and simmer until the fish is flaky and opaque inside, ten to fifteen minutes.
5. Transfer to a serving dish, stir in the cilantro before you serve.

Mustard Fish

Serves 5 pax

Ingredients

- 1/2 teaspoon salt, or to taste
- 3 green chile peppers, such as serrano, chopped lengthwise
- 1/4 cup crudely ground black mustard seeds
- 1/4 teaspoon ground turmeric
- 2 cups water
- 2 tablespoons mustard oil or vegetable oil
- 7 fresh curry leaves
- A few sprigs fresh cilantro
- 5 pounds any firm fish fillet, such as halibut or swordfish, approximately 3/4 inch thick, cut into 2-inch pieces

Procedure

1. Put the fish pieces in a big non-reactive container, put in the turmeric and salt, and mix thoroughly, ensuring all the pieces are coated thoroughly.
2. Cover using plastic wrap and marinate in the fridge for minimum 1 hour and maximum one day.
3. In a small-sized container, combine the mustard seeds and oil, then add approximately 1/4 cup water to make a paste.
4. Move to a large non-stick wok or saucepan and stir over moderate heat, adding a sprinkling of water every now and then, until the paste is well-cooked, approximately ten minutes.
5. Put in the rest of the water and bring to a boil using high heat. Put in the fish and any juices that might have collected in the container, and boil once more.
6. Put in the green chile peppers and curry leaves. Decrease the heat to moderate to low and simmer, turning once, until the fish is just flaky and opaque inside, three to five minutes per side.
7. Move to a serving dish, garnish with the cilantro sprigs before you serve.

New Dheli Fish

Serves 5 pax

Ingredients

- 1 teaspoon ground turmeric
- 2 tablespoons fresh lemon juice
- 1/2 teaspoon salt, or to taste
- 1 cup water
- 1 medium onion, finely chopped
- 5 pounds any firm white fish, such as halibut or sea bass, approximately 3/4-inch thick, cut into 2-inch pieces
- 3 bell peppers (1 red, 1 green, and 1 yellow), cut into 1/2-inch pieces
- A few sprigs fresh cilantro, including soft stems
- 2 tablespoons Bengali 5-Spices (Panch-Phoran)
- 3 tablespoons mustard oil or vegetable oil

Procedure

1. Ready the 5-spice mixture. Put the fish pieces in a big container, put in the turmeric and salt, and mix, ensuring all the pieces are coated thoroughly. Cover and marinate in the fridge 30 to 40 minutes.
2. Heat the oil in a big non-stick wok or saucepan using moderate to high heat and put in the 5-spice mixture; they should sizzle when they touch the hot oil. Swiftly put in the bell peppers and onion, and stir 1 minute.
3. Put in the fish, along with all the marinade, and stir softly to mix. Cook approximately two minutes, then put in the water and bring to a boil using high heat.
4. Decrease the heat to moderate to low, cover the pan, and simmer until the fish is flaky and opaque and the bell peppers are crisp-tender, approximately five to seven minutes.
5. Move to a serving dish, drizzle the lemon juice on top, garnish with the cilantro before you serve.

Onion Fish

Serves 5 pax

Ingredients

- 1/2 teaspoon salt, or to taste
- 1 cup crudely chopped tomatoes
- 1 tablespoon coconut oil or peanut oil
- 1 tablespoon coriander seeds
- 1 tablespoon cumin seeds
- 1/8 teaspoon ground asafoetida
- 1/4 teaspoon ground turmeric
- 1/2 cup Coconut Milk
- 2 pounds firm white fish fillets, such as sea bass or halibut, approximately 3/4 inch thick, cut into 2-inch pieces
- 20 pearl onions, peeled
- 20 fresh curry leaves
- 1/2 cup finely chopped fresh cilantro
- 2 cups water
- 3 fresh green chile peppers, stemmed
- 3 large cloves fresh garlic, peeled

Procedure

1. Ready the coconut milk. Using a blender or a food processor, mix together and pulse the garlic, curry leaves, green chile peppers, cumin, coriander, turmeric, asafoetida, salt, and 1/4 cup coconut milk until a smooth paste is achieved.
2. Heat the oil in a big non-stick wok or saucepan using moderate to high heat and cook the pearl onions, stirring, until a golden color is achieved, approximately four minutes.
3. Put in the garlic-coconut milk paste and cook over moderate heat until it begins to look golden and releases its fragrance, 5 minutes.
4. Put in the fish and cook, turning once, approximately two minutes per side, then put in the rest of the 1/4 cup coconut milk and the cilantro and cook until the oil comes to the sides, approximately two minutes.
5. Put in the water and bring to a boil using high heat.

6. Decrease the heat to moderate to low, cover the pan, and simmer until the sauce is thick and the fish is tender but not breaking apart, approximately five minutes.
7. Move to a serving dish, cover with another dish, and keep warm. To the same pan, put in the tomatoes and cook, stirring, until tender, approximately two minutes.
8. Spread uniformly over the cooked fish as a decoration. Serve hot.

Sesame and Tamarind Fish

Serves 5 pax

Ingredients

- 1/4 cup finely chopped fresh cilantro
- 1/4 cup Tamarind Paste
- 1/4 teaspoon garam masala
- 2 tablespoons white sesame seeds
- 3 tablespoons vegetable oil
- 2 teaspoons cumin seeds
- 1/8 teaspoon ground asafoetida
- 1/4 cup finely chopped dried coconut (kopra)
- 2 pounds any firm fish fillets, 1/2 inch thick, cut
- 2 tablespoons coriander seeds
- 2 cups water
- 1/2 teaspoon fenugreek seeds
- 1/2 teaspoon hot red pepper flakes, or to taste
- 1 small head garlic, cloves separated but not peeled
- 1 teaspoon salt, or to taste
- 15 to 20 fresh curry leaves
- 2 medium onions, with skin on, halved

Procedure

1. Ready the tamarind paste. Next, preheat the broiler. Put the onions and garlic on a cookie sheet and broil on the top rack of the oven or in the broiler, flipping over once
2. or twice, until thoroughly charred. Allow to cool, peel off most of the charred skin from the onions (leave a little of the second layer for flavour) and garlic, then process using a food processor or a blender until a smooth paste is achieved. Leave in the work container.
3. In a small-sized non-stick skillet over moderate heat, dry-roast together the coconut, sesame seeds, and red pepper flakes until a golden color is achieved and remove to a container.
4. Next, dry-roast the coriander, 2 teaspoons cumin, and fenugreek seeds until seems slightly darker.
5. Allow to cool, then grind all the dry-roasted ingredients together in a spice or a coffee grinder to make as fine as possible.
6. Put into the roasted onion-garlic paste and process once again to mix.

7. Heat the oil in a big non-stick wok or saucepan using moderate to high heat and put in the rest of the 1 teaspoon cumin seeds; they should sizzle when they touch the hot oil.
8. Swiftly put in the curry leaves and asafoetida, then cautiously (in case it splatters) stir in the processed onion-spice paste.
9. Cook, stirring as required, over moderate heat until a golden brown colour is achieved, approximately ten minutes.
10. Stir in the tamarind paste and cook approximately two minutes. Put in the fish pieces and salt and stir cautiously approximately two minutes.
11. Next, put in the water and cilantro and simmer until the fish is flaky and opaque and the oil comes to the sides, approximately ten minutes.
12. Move to a serving dish, sprinkle the garam masala on top before you serve.

Spicy Coconut Fish

Serves 5 pax

Ingredients

- 1 (1-inch) piece peeled ginger, cut into matchsticks
- 1 large onion, chopped
- 1 small onion, crudely chopped
- 1 tablespoon coriander seeds
- 2 pounds any firm fish fillets, such as halibut, salmon, or swordfish, cut into 2 inches pieces
- 2 large cloves fresh garlic, peeled
- 5 tablespoons peanut oil
- 1/4 cup chopped fresh cilantro, including soft stems 1/4 teaspoon ground turmeric
- 1/2 cup Coconut Milk
- 1/2 teaspoon salt, or to taste
- 1 tablespoon distilled white vinegar
- 1 teaspoon black mustard seeds
- 1 teaspoon black peppercorns
- 6 dried red chile peppers, broken into pieces

Procedure

1. Ready the coconut milk. Next, in a small spice or coffee grinder, crudely mix together and grind the red chile peppers, coriander, mustard seeds, and the peppercorns.
2. Using a food processor or a blender, combine and pulse the chopped onion and garlic until the desired smoothness is achieved. P
3. ut in the ground spice mixture, the turmeric, and the salt and process once again until a smooth paste is achieved.
4. Put the fish pieces in a big non-reactive container, put in the marinade, and mix thoroughly, ensuring that all the pieces are coated thoroughly.
5. Cover using plastic wrap and marinate in the fridge for minimum 1 and maximum four hours.
6. Heat half of the oil in a big non-stick skillet over moderate heat and cook the chopped onion and ginger, stirring, until browned, approximately seven minutes. Move to a container.

7. Put in the rest of the oil to the skillet and fry the fish pieces, flipping over once or twice, until a golden color is achieved outside, approximately four minutes total.
8. Put in the coconut milk and simmer over low heat, approximately five minutes. Do not stir using a spoon; if required, stir by shaking the skillet.
9. Super cautiously, stir in the vinegar and simmer another two to three minutes to blend the flavors. (The fish should be just flaky and opaque inside.)
10. Move to a serving dish, sprinkle the cilantro on top before you serve.

Halibut with Yogurt and Cashew Sauce

Serves 5 pax

Ingredients

- 1/4 teaspoon ground turmeric
- 1/4 teaspoon salt, or to taste
- 1/2 teaspoon garam masala
- 1 cup non-fat plain yogurt, whisked until the desired smoothness is achieved
- 3 tablespoons peanut oil
- 6 quarter-size slices peeled fresh ginger
- 1/4 cup chickpea flour
- 1/4 teaspoon ground green cardamom seeds
- 1/4 teaspoon ground paprika
- 1 cup water
- 2 pounds halibut fillets, 1 inch thick, cut
- 2 large cloves fresh garlic, peeled
- 1 large onion, finely chopped
- 1 tablespoon minced fresh garlic
- 3 green chile peppers, stemmed
- 3 tablespoons ground raw cashews

Procedure

1. Ready the garam masala. Put the fish in a container. combine the chickpea flour,
2. minced garlic, turmeric, paprika (or cayenne pepper), cardamom seeds, and salt and add to the fish. Toss softly to combine, ensuring each piece is coated thoroughly with this mixture.
3. Cover using plastic wrap and marinate in the fridge for minimum 1 and maximum one day.
4. In the meantime, make the curry. Using a food processor or a blender, combine and pulse the ground cashews, garlic cloves, ginger, green chile peppers, and 1/2 cup yogurt until the desired smoothness is achieved. Move to a container.
5. Next, process the rest of the 1/2 cup yogurt with 1 cup water until the desired smoothness is achieved.
6. Heat 2 tablespoons oil in a big non-stick skillet using high heat and cook the onion, stirring, until browned, approximately ten minutes.
7. Put in the yogurt-cashew paste and continue to cook until all the fluids vaporize, approximately five minutes.

8. Put in the yogurt-water mixture and bring to a boil using high heat. Decrease the heat to moderate to low, cover the pan, and simmer until the sauce is thick and smooth, approximately ten minutes. Move to an ovenproof dish.
9. Preheat your oven 400°F. To the pan Put in the rest of the 1 tablespoon oil and the fish pieces (in 2 batches, if required) and fry, turning gently, until the fish is golden on all sides, approximately five minutes per batch. Put into the sauce and mix gently.
10. Sprinkle the garam masala on top, cover the dish, and bake approximately ten minutes to blend the flavors.
11. Serve hot.

Coconut Fish

Serves 5 pax

Ingredients

- 1/2 teaspoon salt, or to taste
- 1 large onion, finely chopped
- 1 teaspoon black mustard seeds
- 1 teaspoon ground black mustard seeds
- 1/4 cup hot water
- 1/4 teaspoon ground turmeric
- 1/3 cup Coconut Milk
- 5 pounds any firm fish fillets, approximately 3/4 inches thick, cut into 2-inch pieces
- 5 tablespoons coconut oil
- 3 dried red chile peppers, broken into pieces
- 3 fresh green chile peppers, stemmed
- 2 cups of water
- 4 large cloves fresh garlic, peeled
- 5 crudely chopped kokum halves
- 4 quarter-size slices peeled fresh ginger
- 8 fresh green curry leaves, lightly crumpled

Procedure

1. Ready the coconut milk. Put the fish in a container, put in the turmeric and salt, and mix thoroughly, ensuring all the fish pieces are coated thoroughly.
2. Cover and marinate in the fridge for approximately 1 hour. In the meantime, soak the chopped kokum in the hot water for approximately half an hour.
3. Using a blender or a food processor, combine and pulse the kokum, plus the water they were soaking in, the green and red chile peppers, ginger, garlic, and ground mustard seeds until a smooth paste is achieved.
4. Heat the oil in large non-stick skillet using moderate to high heat and put in the whole mustard seeds; they should splatter on contact with the hot oil, so cover the pan until the splattering diminishes.
5. Swiftly put in the onion, decrease the heat to moderate to low, cover the pan, and cook until the onion is soft but not golden, approximately eight to ten minutes.

6. Put in the kokum, ginger-garlic paste and cook over moderate heat, stirring, three to five minutes. Put in the fish and 2 cups water and bring to a boil using high heat. Decrease the heat to low, cover the pan, and cook approximately five minutes.
7. Put in the coconut milk and curry leaves and simmer until the sauce is thick and the fish is tender, just flaky and opaque inside, approximately five minutes, pouring in additional water if you want a thinner sauce. Do not stir the fish at all. To mix, swirl the pan a little on the burner.
8. Move to a serving dish and serve hot.

Mediterranean Fish Recipes

North African Monkfish Tagine

Serves 5 pax

Ingredients

- 1 large onion, halved and sliced 1/4 inch thick
- 1 tablespoon tomato paste
- 1 teaspoon ground cumin
- 1 teaspoon sherry vinegar
- 1/4 cup pitted oil-cured black olives, quartered
- 1/4 teaspoon saffron threads, crumbled
- 1/2 teaspoon dried mint
- 5 (2-inch) strips orange zest
- 3 carrots, peeled, sliced 1/4 inch thick
- 5 garlic cloves, minced
- 1 (8-ounce) bottle clam juice
- 2 teaspoons paprika
- 2 pounds skinless monkfish fillets, 2 inches thick
- 3 tablespoons extra-virgin olive oil
- 2 tablespoons minced fresh mint
- Salt and pepper

Procedure

1. Mince 1 strip orange zest and combine with 1 teaspoon garlic in a container; set aside.
2. Heat oil in a Dutch oven on moderate heat until it starts to shimmer. Put in onion, carrots, 1/4 teaspoon salt, and remaining 2 strips orange zest and cook until vegetables are softened and lightly browned, 10 to 12 minutes.
3. Mix in remaining garlic, tomato paste, paprika, cumin, dried mint, and saffron and cook until aromatic, approximately half a minute. Mix in clam juice, scraping up any browned bits.
4. Pat monkfish dry using paper towels and sprinkle with salt and pepper. Nestle monkfish into pot, spoon some cooking liquid over top, and bring to simmer.
5. Decrease heat to moderate to low, cover, and simmer gently until monkfish is opaque in center and registers 160 degrees, 8 to 12 minutes.
6. Discard orange zest. Gently mix in olives, fresh mint, vinegar, and garlic–orange zest mixture.
7. Sprinkle with salt and pepper to taste. Serve.

Zesty Hake Fillets

Serves 4 pax

Ingredients

- 2 pounds russet potatoes, unpeeled, sliced into 1/4-inch-thick rounds
- 2 garlic cloves, minced
- 4 (4- to 6-ounce) skinless hake fillets, 2 inches thick
- 1/4 cup extra-virgin olive oil
- 1 lemon, sliced thin
- 4 sprigs fresh thyme
- Salt and pepper

Procedure

1. Place oven rack to lower-middle position and preheat your oven to 425 degrees. Toss potatoes with 2 tablespoons oil and garlic in a container and sprinkle with salt and pepper.
2. Microwave, uncovered, until potatoes are just tender, 12 to 14 minutes, stirring halfway through microwaving.
3. Move potatoes to 13 by 9-inch baking dish and press gently into even layer. Pat hake dry using paper towels, sprinkle with salt and pepper, and arrange skinned side down on top of potatoes.
4. Sprinkle hake with remaining 2 tablespoons oil, then place thyme sprigs and lemon slices on top.
5. Bake until hake flakes apart when softly poked using paring knife and registers 140 degrees, fifteen to twenty minutes.
6. Slide spatula underneath potatoes and hake and carefully move to individual plates.
7. Serve.

Citric Scallops

Serves 5 pax

Ingredients

- 1 tablespoon minced fresh cilantro
- 2 pounds large sea scallops, tendons removed
- 1/8 teaspoon red pepper flakes
- 2 tablespoons orange juice
- 6 tablespoons extra-virgin olive oil
- 1 small shallot, minced
- 3 tablespoons lime juice
- Salt and pepper

Procedure

1. Place scallops in rimmed baking sheet lined with clean kitchen towel. Place second clean kitchen towel on top of scallops and press gently on towel to blot liquid. Let scallops sit at room temperature, covered with towel, for about ten minutes.
2. Beat 1/4 cup oil, orange juice, lime juice, shallot, cilantro, and pepper flakes together in a container. Sprinkle with salt to taste and set aside for serving.
3. Heat 1 tablespoon oil in 12-inch non-stick frying pan on moderate to high heat until just smoking.
4. Put in half of scallops to frying pan in one layer and cook, without moving them, until thoroughly browned on first side, about 2 minutes.
5. Flip scallops and continue to cook, without moving them, until thoroughly browned on second side, about 2 minutes.
6. Move scallops to serving platter and tent loosely with aluminium foil. Repeat with residual 1 tablespoon oil and remaining scallops.
7. Beat dressing to recombine and serve with scallops.

Steamed Mussels

Serves 5 pax

Ingredients

- 2 tablespoons minced fresh parsley
- 2 garlic cloves, minced
- 3 sprigs fresh thyme
- 5 tablespoons extra-virgin olive oil
- 1/4 teaspoon salt
- 1 cup dry white wine
- 2 bay leaves
- 12 pounds mussels, scrubbed and debearded
- Pinch red pepper flakes

Procedure

1. Place oven rack on the lowest position and pre-heat your oven to 500 degrees.
2. Heat 1 tablespoon oil, garlic, and pepper flakes in large roasting pan on moderate heat and cook, stirring continuously, until aromatic, approximately half a minute.
3. Mix in wine, thyme sprigs, and bay leaves, bring to boil, and cook until wine is slightly reduced, approximately one minute.
4. Mix in mussels and salt. Cover pan tightly with aluminium foil and move to oven. Cook until most mussels have opened (a few may remain closed), fifteen to twenty minutes.
5. Remove pan from oven. Discard thyme sprigs, bay leaves, and any mussels that refuse to open.
6. Sprinkle with remaining 2 tablespoons oil, drizzle with parsley, and toss to combine.
7. Serve.

Roasted Garlic Shrimp

Serves 5 pax

Ingredients

- 1/2 teaspoon red pepper flakes
- 1 teaspoon anise seeds
- 12 pounds shell-on jumbo shrimp (16 to 20 per pound)
- 2 tablespoons minced fresh parsley
- 1/4 cup extra-virgin olive oil
- 1/4 cup salt
- 1/4 teaspoon pepper
- 6 garlic cloves, minced
- 5 Lemon wedges

Procedure

1. Dissolve salt in 4 cups cold water in large container. Using kitchen shears or
2. sharp paring knife, cut through shell of shrimp and devein but do not remove shell. Use a paring knife to continue to cut shrimp 1/2 inch deep, taking care not to cut in half fully.
3. Immerse shrimp in brine, cover, put inside your fridge for about fifteen minutes.
4. Place oven rack 4 inches from broiler element and heat broiler. Mix oil, garlic, anise seeds, pepper flakes, and pepper in a big container.
5. Remove shrimp from brine and pat dry using paper towels. Put in shrimp and parsley to oil mixture and toss well, making sure oil mixture gets into interior of shrimp. Arrange shrimp in one layer on wire rack set in rimmed baking sheet.
6. Broil shrimp until opaque and shells are starting to brown, 2 to 4 minutes, rotating sheet halfway through broiling.

7. Flip shrimp and continue to broil until second side is opaque and shells are starting to brown, 2 to 4 minutes, rotating sheet halfway through broiling.
8. Serve with lemon wedges.

Tangy Roasted Snapper

Serves 4 pax

Ingredients

- 2 teaspoons grated lime zest plus 2 tablespoons juice
- 1/8 teaspoon red pepper flakes
- 6 tablespoons extra-virgin olive oil
- Salt and pepper
- 4 (2-pound) whole red snapper, scaled, gutted, fins snipped off with scissors
- 1/4 cup minced fresh cilantro
- 1 small shallot, minced
- 2 teaspoons grated orange zest plus 2 tablespoons juice

Procedure

1. Place the oven rack in the center of the oven and pre-heat your oven to 500 degrees. Line rimmed baking sheet with parchment paper and grease parchment.
2. Beat 1/4 cup oil, cilantro, lime juice, orange juice, shallot, and pepper flakes together in a container.
3. Sprinkle with salt and pepper to taste; set aside for serving.
4. In a different container, combine lime zest, orange zest, 2 teaspoons salt, and 1/2 teaspoon pepper.
5. Wash each snapper under cold running water and pat dry using paper towels inside and out. Using sharp knife, make 3 or 4 shallow slashes, about 2 inches apart, on both sides of snapper.
6. Open cavity of each snapper and drizzle 1 teaspoon salt mixture on flesh. Brush 1 tablespoon oil on outside of each snapper and season with remaining salt mixture; move to readied sheet and allow to sit for about ten minutes.

7. Roast until snapper flakes apart when softly poked using paring knife and registers 140 degrees, fifteen to twenty minutes. (To check for doneness, peek into slashed flesh or into interior through opened bottom area of each fish.)
8. Cautiously move snapper to carving board and allow to rest for about five minutes. Fillet snapper by making vertical cut just behind head from top of fish to belly.
9. Make another cut along top of snapper from head to tail. Use spatula to lift meat from bones, starting at head end and running spatula over bones to lift out fillet.
10. Repeat on other side of snapper. Discard head and skeleton.
11. Beat dressing to recombine and serve with snapper.

Spanish Mix

Serves 5 pax

Ingredients

- 2 pounds leeks, white and light green parts only, halved along the length, sliced thin, and washed
- 5 cups pearl couscous
- 5 tablespoons extra-virgin olive oil
- 1/2 cup minced fresh parsley
- 1 cup dry vermouth or dry white wine
- 1 tablespoon minced fresh thyme
- 2 garlic cloves, minced
- 5 tomatoes, cored, seeded, and chopped
- 10 pounds littleneck clams, scrubbed
- 6 ounces Spanish-style chorizo sausage, halved along the length and sliced thin
- Salt and pepper

Procedure

1. Bring 2 quarts water to boil in moderate-sized saucepan. Mix in couscous and 2 teaspoons salt and cook until al dente, approximately eight minutes; drain.
2. In the meantime, heat oil in a Dutch oven on moderate heat. Put in leeks and chorizo and cook until leeks are tender, about 4 minutes.
3. Mix in garlic and thyme and cook until aromatic, approximately half a minute. Mix in vermouth and cook until slightly reduced, approximately one minute. Mix in tomatoes and clams, cover, and cook until clams open, 8 to 12 minutes.
4. Use slotted spoon to move clams to large serving bowl, discarding any that refuse to open. Stir couscous and parsley into cooking liquid and sprinkle with salt and pepper to taste.
5. Portion couscous mixture into individual bowls, top with clams, and serve.

Spanish Shellfish Stew

Serves 5 pax

Ingredients

- 1 (28-ounce) can whole peeled tomatoes, chopped
- 1 onion, chopped fine
- 1 recipe Picada
- 1 red bell pepper, stemmed, seeded, and chopped
- 1/8 teaspoon red pepper flakes
- 1/4 cup extra-virgin olive oil
- 1/4 teaspoon saffron threads, crumbled
- 1 tablespoon minced fresh parsley
- 12 ounces large sea scallops, tendons removed
- 2 bay leaves
- 5 tablespoons brandy
- 2 garlic cloves, minced
- 1 teaspoon paprika
- 2 cups dry white wine or dry vermouth
- 2 pounds littleneck clams, scrubbed
- 8 ounces medium-large shrimp (40 per pound)
- 8 ounces mussels, scrubbed and debearded

Procedure

1. Heat 1 tablespoon oil in moderate-sized saucepan on moderate heat until it starts to shimmer. Put in shrimp shells and cook, stirring often, until they begin to turn spotty brown and pot starts to brown, 2 to 4 minutes. Remove from the heat, mix in wine, cover, and allow to steep until ready to use.
2. Heat remaining 3 tablespoons oil in large Dutch oven on moderate to high heat until it starts to shimmer. Put in onion and bell pepper and cook till they become tender and lightly browned, 5 to 7 minutes.
3. Mix in garlic, paprika, saffron, and pepper flakes and cook until aromatic, approximately half a minute. Mix in brandy, scraping up any browned bits. Mix in tomatoes and their juice and bay leaves and cook until slightly thickened, 5 to 7 minutes.
4. Strain wine mixture into Dutch oven, pressing on solids to extract as much liquid as possible; discard solids. Bring to simmer and cook until flavors blend, 3 to 5 minutes.

5. Nestle clams into pot, cover, and cook for 4 minutes. Nestle mussels and scallops into pot, cover, and carry on cooking until most clams have opened, approximately three minutes.
6. Arrange shrimp uniformly over stew, cover, and carry on cooking until shrimp are opaque throughout, scallops are firm and opaque in center, and clams and mussels have opened, 1 to 2 minutes.
7. Remove from the heat, discard bay leaves and any clams and mussels that refuse to open. Mix in picada and parsley and sprinkle with salt and pepper to taste.
8. Serve in wide, shallow bowls with lemon wedges.

Greek Stuffed Squid

Serves 4 pax

Ingredients

- 1/2 cup plain dried breadcrumbs
- 1 (15-ounce) can tomato sauce
- 1 garlic clove, minced
- 1/4 cup golden raisins
- 1/4 cup pine nuts, toasted
- 1/2 cup dry white wine
- 4 anchovy fillets, rinsed and minced
- 2 tablespoons minced fresh parsley
- 1 tablespoon dried mint
- 16 medium squid bodies, plus 6 ounces tentacles, chopped
- 5 tablespoons extra-virgin olive oil
- 2 onions, chopped fine
- Salt and pepper

Procedure

1. Heat 1 tablespoon oil in 12-inch non-stick frying pan on moderate to high heat until it starts to shimmer.
2. Put in two-thirds of onions and cook till they become tender, approximately five minutes. Mix in squid tentacles and cook until no longer translucent, 1 to 2 minutes.
3. Mix in pine nuts, mint, and 1/4 teaspoon pepper and cook until aromatic, approximately one minute. Move mixture to big container and mix in breadcrumbs, 1/4 cup parsley, raisins, and anchovies.
4. Sprinkle with salt and pepper to taste and allow to cool slightly.
5. Using small soup spoon, portion 2 tablespoons filling into each squid body, pressing on filling gently to create 1-inch space at top. Thread toothpick through opening of each squid to secure closed.

6. Heat residual 1 tablespoon oil in now-empty frying pan on moderate to high heat until it starts to shimmer.
7. Put in remaining onions and cook till they become tender, approximately five minutes. Mix in garlic, 1/4 teaspoon salt, and 1/4 teaspoon pepper and cook until aromatic, approximately half a minute. Mix in wine and tomato sauce and bring to simmer.
8. Nestle squid into sauce. Decrease heat to low, cover, and simmer gently until sauce has thickened slightly and squid is easily pierced with paring knife, about 1 hour, turning squid halfway through cooking.
9. Season sauce with salt and pepper to taste. Remove toothpicks from squid and drizzle with remaining 1 tablespoon parsley.
10. Serve.

Greek Tangy Grilled Squid

Serves 4 pax

Ingredients

- 1 tablespoon lemon juice, plus lemon wedges for serving
- 3 tablespoons baking soda
- 2 teaspoons minced fresh parsley
- 1 garlic clove, minced
- 1 pound small squid
- 5 tablespoons extra-virgin olive oil
- Salt and pepper

Procedure

1. Mix 3 tablespoons oil, lemon juice, parsley, garlic, and 1/4 teaspoon pepper in a big container; set aside for serving.
2. Using kitchen shears, cut squid bodies along the length down one side. Open squid bodies and flatten into planks.
3. Dissolve baking soda and 2 tablespoons salt in 3 cups cold water in large container. Immerse squid bodies and tentacles in brine, cover, put inside your fridge for about fifteen minutes.
4. Remove squid from brine and spread in a uniform layer in rimmed baking sheet lined with clean kitchen towel.
5. Place second clean kitchen towel on top of squid and press gently on towel to blot liquid. Let squid sit at room temperature, covered with towel, for about ten minutes.
6. Toss squid with remaining 2 tablespoons oil and season with pepper. Thread tentacles onto two 12-inch metal skewers.
7.

8. **FOR A GAS GRILL:** Turn all burners to high, cover, and heat grill until hot, about fifteen minutes. Leave all burners on high.
9. Clean cooking grate, then repetitively brush grate with thoroughly oiled paper towels until black and glossy, 5 to 10 times.
10. Place squid bodies and tentacles on grill (directly over coals if using charcoal), draping long tentacles over skewers to stop them from falling through grates. Cook (covered if using gas) until squid is opaque and mildly charred, approximately five minutes, flipping halfway through cooking.
11. Move bodies to plate and tent loosely with aluminium foil. Continue to grill tentacles until ends become browned and crisp, approximately three minutes; move to plate with bodies.
12. Using tongs, remove tentacles from skewers. Move bodies to slicing board and slice into 1/2-inch-thick strips. Put in tentacles and bodies to a container with oil mixture and toss to coat.
13. Serve with lemon wedges.

Greek-Style Octopus in Red Wine

Serves 4 pax

Ingredients

- 1 tablespoon extra-virgin olive oil
- 2 bay leaves
- 5 tablespoons red wine vinegar
- 2 tablespoons tomato paste
- 2 tablespoons unflavored gelatin
- 1 (4-pound) octopus, rinsed
- 1 cup dry red wine
- Pinch ground cinnamon
- Pinch ground nutmeg
- 1 sprig fresh rosemary
- 2 teaspoons chopped fresh parsley
- 4 garlic cloves, peeled and smashed
- Pepper

Procedure

1. Using sharp knife, separate octopus mantle (large sac) and body (lower section with tentacles) from head (midsection containing eyes); discard head.
2. Place octopus in large pot, cover with water by 2 inches, and bring to simmer on high heat. Decrease heat to low, cover, and simmer gently, flipping octopus occasionally, until skin between tentacle joints tears easily when pulled, 45 minutes to 11/4 hours.
3. Move octopus to slicing board and allow to cool slightly. Measure out and reserve 3 cups octopus cooking liquid; discard remaining liquid and wipe pot dry using paper towels.
4. While octopus is still warm, use paring knife to cut mantle into quarters, then trim and scrape away skin and interior fibers; move to a container.
5. Using your fingers, remove skin from body, being careful not to remove suction cups from tentacles.
6. Cut tentacles from around core of body in three sections; discard core.

7. Separate tentacles and cut into 2-inch lengths; move to a container.
8. Heat oil in now-empty pot on moderate to high heat until it starts to shimmer. Put in tomato paste and cook, stirring continuously, until starting to darken, approximately one minute.
9. Mix in garlic, rosemary sprig, bay leaves, 1/2 teaspoon pepper, cinnamon, and nutmeg and cook until aromatic, approximately half a minute. Mix in reserved octopus cooking liquid, wine, vinegar, and gelatin, scraping up any browned bits. Bring to boil and cook, stirring intermittently, for 20 minutes.
10. Mix in octopus and any accumulated juices and bring to simmer. Cook, stirring intermittently, until octopus becomes soft and sauce has thickened slightly and coats back of spoon, 20 minutes to half an hour.
11. Remove from the heat, discard rosemary sprig and bay leaves. Mix in parsley and season with pepper to taste. Serve.

White Wine Steamed Clams

Serves 5 pax

Ingredients

- 2 tablespoons minced fresh parsley
- 2 shallots, minced
- 3 tablespoons extra-virgin olive oil
- 1 bay leaf
- 2 cups dry white wine
- 2 garlic cloves, minced
- 10 pounds littleneck clams, scrubbed
- Lemon wedges

Procedure

1. Bring wine, shallots, garlic, and bay leaf to simmer in a Dutch oven on high heat and cook for about three minutes.
2. Put in clams, cover, and cook, stirring twice, until clams open, about four to eight minutes. Use a slotted spoon to move clams to serving bowl, discarding any that refuse to open.
3. Remove from the heat, beat oil into cooking liquid until combined. Pour sauce over clams and drizzle with parsley.
4. Serve with lemon wedges.

Calamari Stew

Serves 5 pax

Ingredients

- 1/4 cup extra-virgin olive oil, plus extra for serving
- 1/4 teaspoon red pepper flakes
- 1/3 cup pitted brine-cured green olives, chopped
- 1/2 cup dry white wine or dry vermouth
- 1 tablespoon capers, rinsed
- 2 celery ribs, sliced thin
- 2 onions, chopped fine
- 12 pounds small squid, bodies sliced crosswise into 1-inch-thick rings, tentacles halved
- 2 (28-ounce) cans whole peeled tomatoes, drained and chopped coarse
- 3 tablespoons minced fresh parsley
- 8 garlic cloves, minced
- Salt and pepper

Procedure

1. Heat oil in a Dutch oven on moderate to high heat until it starts to shimmer. Put in onions and celery and cook till they become tender, approximately five minutes. Mix in garlic and pepper flakes and cook until aromatic, approximately half a minute. Mix in wine, scraping up any browned bits, and cook until nearly evaporated, approximately one minute.
2. Pat squid dry using paper towels and sprinkle with salt and pepper. Stir squid into pot. Decrease heat to moderate to low, cover, and simmer gently until squid has released its liquid, about fifteen minutes. Mix in tomatoes, olives, and capers, cover, and carry on cooking until squid is very tender, 30 to 35 minutes.
3. Remove from the heat, mix in parsley and sprinkle with salt and pepper to taste.
4. Serve, drizzling individual portions with extra oil.

Zesty Hake Fillets

Serves 4 pax

Ingredients

- 2 garlic cloves, minced
- 4 (4- to 6-ounce) skinless hake fillets, 2 inches thick
- 1/4 cup extra-virgin olive oil
- 1 lemon, sliced thin
- 2 pounds russet potatoes, unpeeled, sliced into 1/4-inch-thick rounds
- 4 sprigs fresh thyme
- Salt and pepper

Procedure

8. Place oven rack to lower-middle position and preheat your oven to 425 degrees. Toss potatoes with 2 tablespoons oil and garlic in a container and sprinkle with salt and pepper.
9. Microwave, uncovered, until potatoes are just tender, 12 to 14 minutes, stirring halfway through microwaving.
10. Move potatoes to 13 by 9-inch baking dish and press gently into even layer. Pat hake dry using paper towels, sprinkle with salt and pepper, and arrange skinned side down on top of potatoes.
11. Sprinkle hake with remaining 2 tablespoons oil, then place thyme sprigs and lemon slices on top.
12. Bake until hake flakes apart when softly poked using paring knife and registers 140 degrees, fifteen to twenty minutes. Slide spatula underneath potatoes and hake and carefully move to individual plates.
13. Serve.

Sautéed Sole

Serves 4 pax

Ingredients

- 8 (2- to 3-ounce) skinless sole fillets, 1/4 to 1/2 inch thick
- 1/4 cup extra-virgin olive oil
- 1/2 cup all-purpose flour
- 4 Lemon wedges
- Salt and pepper

Procedure

1. Place flour in shallow dish. Pat sole dry using paper towels and sprinkle with salt and pepper.
2. Working with 1 fillet at a time, dredge in flour to coat, shaking off any excess.
3. Heat 2 tablespoons oil in 12-inch non-stick frying pan on moderate to high heat until it starts to shimmer.
4. Place half of sole in frying pan and cook until lightly browned on first side, 2 to 3 minutes. Gently flip sole using 2 spatulas and carry on cooking until fish flakes apart when softly poked using paring knife, 30 to 60 seconds.
5. Cautiously move sole to serving platter and tent loosely with aluminium foil.
6. Wipe frying pan clean using paper towels and repeat with remaining 2 tablespoons oil and fillets.
7. Serve with lemon wedges.

Thank you, dear fish lover.

I am glad you accepted my teachings.
These meals have been personally codified in my worldwide trips.
I wanted to share them with you, to let people know more about meat and how to treat it properly.

Now you had come to know about Indian and Mediterranean Fish in all of its shapes, let me give you one more tip.
This manual takes part of an unmissable cookbooks collection.
These fish-based recipes, mixed to all the tastes I met around the world, will give you a complete idea of the possibilities this world offers to us.
You have now the opportunity to add hundreds new elements to your cooking skills knowledge.
Check out the other books!

Ernest Pescara

Lightning Source UK Ltd.
Milton Keynes UK
UKHW022105110621
385375UK00002B/405

9 781802 943986